How Coyote Stole the Summer

Adapted by Stephen Krensky
Illustrations by Kelly Dupre

A
NATIVE
AMERICAN
FOLKTALE

On My Own

FOLKLORE

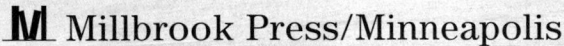
M Millbrook Press/Minneapolis

Special thanks to Glenda Trosper, Director of the Eastern Shoshone Tribal Cultural Center, Fort Washakie, Wyoming, for serving as a consultant on this title.

Text copyright © 2009 by Stephen Krensky
Illustrations copyright © 2009 by Lerner Publishing Group, Inc.

Millbrook Press
A division of Lerner Publishing Group, Inc.
241 First Avenue North
Minneapolis, MN 55401 U.S.A.

Website address: www.lernerbooks.com

Library of Congress Cataloging-in-Publication Data

Krensky, Stephen.
    How Coyote stole the summer / adapted by Stephen Krensky ; illustrated by Kelly Dupre.
      p.   cm. — (On my own folklore)
    ISBN: 978–0–8225–7548–1 (lib. bdg. : alk. paper)
    1. Indians of North America—Folklore. 2. Coyote (Legendary character)—Legends.
I. Dupre, Kelly, ill. II. Title.
E98.F6K743 2009
398.2089'97—dc22   2007015951

Manufactured in the United States of America
1 2 3 4 5 6 – DP – 14 13 12 11 10 09

For Andrew,
who likes summer all year round —S.K.

To Mom, who showed me
the beautiful connection
between art and cultures
the world over —K.D.

The Endless Winter

Back at the beginning of time,

Old Man Coyote was cold.

He wasn't cold some of the time.

He wasn't cold most of the time.

He was cold all the time.

4

The weather ranged from cold
to very cold to freezing cold.
Old Man Coyote spent his days
shivering and shuddering.
Icicles hung from his nose
and his toes.
Frost covered his fur
from head to tail.
And he couldn't do anything about it.

One morning, Coyote woke up
covered with a blanket of fresh snow.
As he shook it off,
he thought he heard some ice cracking
above him.
"CRRAAACCCCCKKKLE."
Then he looked up.
The sound came from Raven.
He was cackling over Coyote's head.
"What are you laughing about?"
asked Coyote.
"Every time I see you,
you are laughing at me."
"That's because you're so funny,"
said Raven.
"Here you are suffering in the cold
when you could be nice and warm."
"I could?" said Coyote.

The raven nodded.

"Listen closely.

Far from here is a tipi where

Old Woman and her children live.

Old Woman has a special gift

that she keeps in a black bag.

This gift is called summer.

She will not share it with anyone.

But if you could get this summer,

you would be warm at last."

Old Man Coyote

eyed Raven suspiciously.

"In that case," he said, "why haven't

you taken summer for yourself?"

"Ah," said Raven, "I wish I could.

But this Old Woman is powerful.

A bird like me would have no

chance against her."

"But I am only a single animal," said Coyote.
"Why are my chances any better?"
"You cannot do it alone," Raven admitted.
"You must take five other animals
with you—a wolf, a moose, a stag,
an elk, and an antelope.
You will also need this powerful
medicine that I will give you."
Old Man Coyote wasn't sure
if he should believe Raven.

But what if there was really a chance for him to be nice and warm? That was a chance worth taking.

Coyote went to see the other animals

Raven had mentioned.

They were all just as cold as he was.

Coyote told them what Raven had said.

They too were a little suspicious.

But the idea of getting warm
was too tempting to resist.
So they agreed to help.
"Raven and I have a plan," said Coyote.
Then he explained what everyone
would need to do.

The Plan Unfolds

Coyote and Wolf crept up to a hill
and carefully looked over the top.
They saw the tipi where Old Woman
lived with her many children.
"It is time," Coyote whispered.
Wolf stepped out into the clearing.
Then he began to howl.

Old Woman's children looked around.

Who was making that noise?

"It's a wolf," said one.

"We must catch him," said another.

"And cook him," said a third.

"And eat him," said a fourth.

They started to chase after Wolf,
who ran away as fast as he could.
Coyote smiled.
With the children gone,
there was no one to stop him.

Slowly, carefully, he crept up
to the flap of the tipi.
Then Coyote poked his head inside.
There he saw Old Woman.
She was busy making moccasins
and humming to herself.
Suddenly, she stopped.
"Who's there?" she asked.
In a flash, Coyote leaped forward.
He smeared Raven's medicine
on Old Woman's lips.
She cried out,
but no words escaped her mouth.
The medicine had magically
removed her voice.

Coyote looked around and saw
a black bag sitting on the ground.
He grabbed it
and darted out of the tent.
Old Woman still could not speak,
but she rushed outside
and put a pine branch over her fire.
It sent a great plume of smoke into the air.

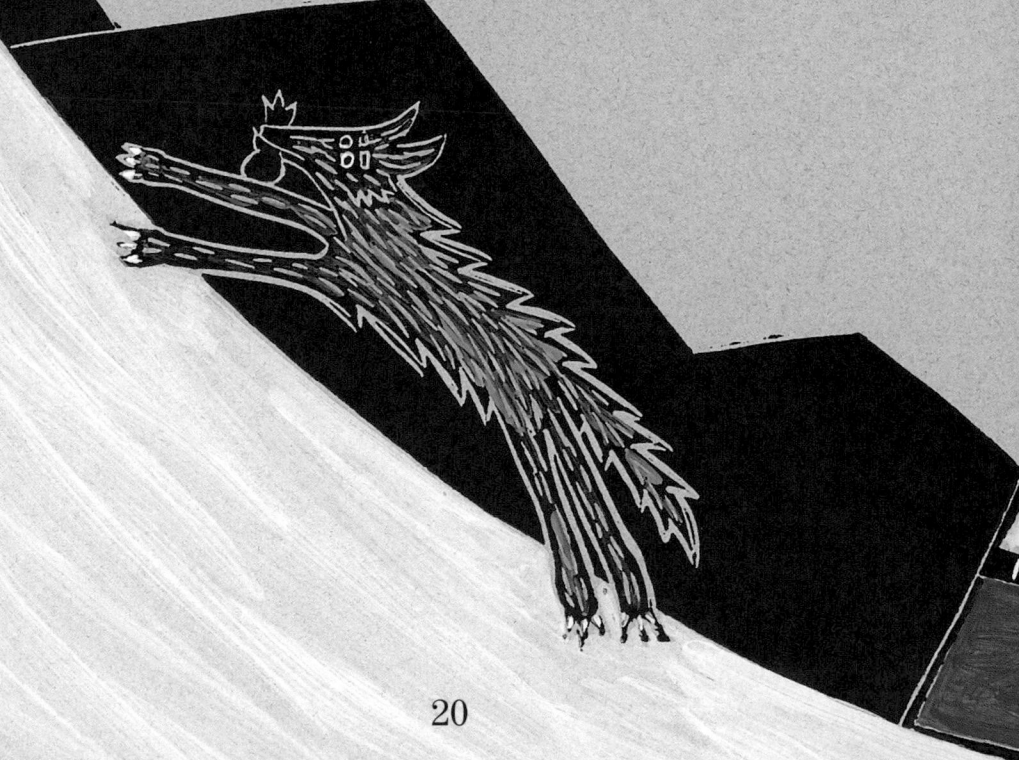

Old Woman's children saw
the smoke from a distance.
They knew at once
that something was wrong.
They stopped chasing Wolf
and hurried home.
They got there just in time to see Coyote
running away with the black bag.

Their mother was waving
and jumping up and down.
She didn't need to say a word.
Her children could see what had happened.
"Stop, thief!" they shouted.
Then they ran after Coyote
as fast as they could.

The Chase

Coyote was fast.
He bounded across the plains
holding the bag between his teeth.
But every time he looked back,
Old Woman's children
were getting closer and closer.

If Coyote had been alone,
Old Woman's children
surely would have caught him.
But luckily, he was not alone.

Over the next hill, he reached
the place where Moose was waiting.
"Go, go, go!" he gasped,
passing the bag to Moose.
And Moose trotted off
on her fresh legs.
Coyote turned to face
Old Woman's children.

But they ran past him
without even a look.
All they cared about
was getting the bag back.
Moose ran through the brush.
The bushes did not bother her,
but they slowed down
Old Woman's children for a while.
Then they began to catch up.

They were almost on Moose

when she reached the place

where Stag was waiting.

"Your turn!" said Moose,

dropping to the ground.

Stag grabbed the bag and ran on.

Old Woman's children ignored Moose

and kept their eyes on Stag.

By now, though,

they had been running a long time.

They were strong and fast,

but they were not tireless.

Even so, they slowly gained on Stag.

Just as they were catching up again,
Stag reached Elk
and passed the bag off to her.
"Off with you!" said Stag.
Elk was faster than Stag.

30

Old Woman's children
were panting hard
as they continued the chase.
They kept pace with Elk for a while.
But as fast as they ran,
they could not catch her.

When Stag got tired,

he met up with Antelope,

who was the fastest of all.

"Go catch the wind!" said Stag,
passing the bag along.
And Antelope bounded off.

The sight of Antelope was a blow
to Old Woman's children.
They had run as far as their legs
and hearts could carry them.

34

They hated to admit defeat,
but Antelope pulled farther
and farther away.
Finally, the children came to a stop.

A New Season Begins

Antelope saw that the children
had stopped following her.
So she made her way back
to Coyote's village.
There she waited
for the other animals to arrive.
Elk was first, followed by Stag,
Moose, and Wolf.
Flying overhead was Raven,
cackling the whole time.
Coyote was the last to get back.
The others gave him the honor
of opening the bag.

"Let's see what all this trouble
has gotten us," said Coyote.
As he opened the bag,
summer jumped out
like a great gust of wind.
The animals could feel it at once.
The icicles and frost melted away,
leaving behind great puddles.

All around them, colors spread over
the landscape.
Flowers bloomed in seconds.
Leaves seemed to burst out
of the tree branches.
The grass turned green
as far as the animals could see.

But the animals had forgotten
one thing.
With summer breaking out,
it wasn't hard for Old Woman
and her children to track them down.
And they appeared quickly.
"You are a thief!" Old Woman
shouted at Coyote.
"You and your friends have stolen
summer from our mother,"
said her children.
"You need to give it back."
"I will not," said Coyote.
"Summer is too precious
to be sealed up in a bag.
It should be shared by everyone."

"If you do not give it back,"
said Old Woman's children,
"we will make war upon you."
Old Man Coyote wanted to be warm,
but he did not want to fight in a war.
The other animals felt the same.
"I have an idea," said Coyote.
"Why don't we share summer
between us?

You can have it
for half of the year.
And we will have it for the other."

Old Woman and her children
stopped to think.
They were still angry.
But they knew that going to war
would not make them feel any better.
And they too liked how summer felt,
now that it was out in the open air.
"That is fair," they said finally.

And so the animals
and Old Woman's family
have shared the summer
between them ever since.

Afterword

Coyotes live all over North America, from Canada to the United States to Mexico. But this wasn't always the case. Hundreds of years ago, most coyotes lived on the plains and deserts of central and western North America. The Native American groups in these areas tell many stories about coyotes.

In stories, coyotes are often tricksters. A trickster is a character who plays tricks to do certain tasks. Tricksters often break the rules. Sometimes they play tricks to do something good, such as sharing summer with everyone. Other times, a trickster might play a mean trick on someone else.

The story in this book is set in Wyoming, where the Eastern Shoshones live. The illustrations show the Wyoming landscape, with grassy plains and the Rocky Mountains in the background. The style of the tipi and the clothing Old Woman and her children wear are similar to traditional Shoshone tipis and clothing.

Native American groups such as Shastas, Hupas, and Shoshones all tell stories about a coyote stealing something. But the stories are not all the same. For example, in some versions, Coyote steals fire from the old woman instead of stealing summer. In other versions, the coyote steals daylight. The animals that help him are also different in different stories. In a Shasta story, the helpers are a squirrel, a chipmunk, and a frog.

Native American stories did not start out being written in books. People learned the stories by hearing other people tell them out loud. Every storyteller might tell a story a little bit differently. If you were telling this story to a friend, how would you tell it?

Glossary

blow: a disappointment

brush: an area with many small trees and bushes

cackling: laughing

defeat: losing or being beaten

moccasins: soft leather shoes

plume: a long column of smoke

shuddering: shaking

stag: an adult male deer

suspiciously: not trustingly

tipi: a cone-shaped home made of tall wooden poles and covered with animal skins

Further Reading and Websites

BOOKS

Hausman, Gerald. *Coyote Walks on Two Legs: A Book of Navajo Myths and Legends*. New York: Philomel Books, 1995.
These five Navajo stories describe Coyote's many adventures. One tale also explains why coyotes have yellow eyes.

London, Jonathan. *Fire Race: A Karuk Coyote Tale*. San Francisco: Chronicle Books, 1993.
Read the Karuk tale of how Coyote steals fire from the Yellow Jacket sisters and shares it with the animal people.

Sonneborn, Liz. *The Shoshones*. Minneapolis: Lerner Publications Company, 2007.
This book gives the history of the Shoshones, from long ago to modern times. It also includes instructions for how to play a traditional Shoshone game.

WEBSITES

Coyote Facts
http://library.thinkquest.org/05aug/00260/fact.html
This website has information about where coyotes live, what they eat, how to identify their paw prints, and much more. If you click on the "fiction" tab at the top of the page, you can find links to coyote folktales online.

Coyote Printout—Enchanted Learning
http://www.enchantedlearning.com/subjects/mammals/dog/Coyoteprintout.shtml
This website has simple facts about coyotes and a diagram with labeled body parts.